COMPASSIONATE LIVING

LIVING

Jackie Hudson

WIPF & STOCK · Eugene, Oregon

Wipf and Stock Publishers
199 W 8th Ave, Suite 3
Eugene, OR 97401

Compassionate Living
By Hudson, Jackie
Copyright©2010 by Hudson, Jackie
ISBN 13: 978-1-60899-502-8
Publication date 3/1/2010

Contents

PREFACE

A young Christian couple sat on the couch across from me. "I can't do this anymore," she cried. "I don't want a divorce, but I have nothing left inside of me but anger and resentment. I'm tired of living under your constant critical eye and your intimidation."

"You! *I* don't understand," the husband snapped. "I make a good living. I come home, and the house isn't clean. You don't have to work. You just have to take care of the two kids and keep the house clean, and you can't even do that. You're always too tired for sex, and I resent that. I can never do enough to please you. I try and try, but it's not enough!"

They both looked at me as the wife spoke through her sobs. "How did we get here? We are both Christians. How did our feelings get so out of control? How can we even *be* Christians and feel this way?"

I've heard hundreds of similar scenarios from sincere Christian couples and individuals who are simply trying their best with what they have to make life work. So many of them have tried everything they know to do—Bible reading, prayer, conferences, spiritual warfare—and yet nothing has changed. One of the biggest struggles they face is the guilt they feel for not being "good enough" Christians to get their feelings in line or make lasting changes in their lives.

Compassionate Living has come out of this struggle. It is an attempt to integrate biblical understanding with current knowledge about emotional life skills and make them accessible to everyday believers on their journeys. It is about the recovery of compassion. Compassion is the key to the healing of our wounded souls and of our fractured, broken world, for it is compassion that moves us to action regarding our own wounds and the wounds of others.

This workbook draws on my own journey to understand and live the Christian life. It has been one of success, failure, heartache, joy, doubt, loss, and hope. It is a journey I have hated and loved. It is a journey that has made me who I am today.

It also draws on many current and past theologians and personality theorists. Their ideas have been filtered through 40 years of my own growth and understanding, making it difficult to cite individual sources.

Two charts, "A Biblical Growth Model" and "The PRAY Process," come from my collaboration with Carolyn Rexius, LCSW, during the years we worked together (1996–2002). I have changed some of the wording on the Biblical Growth Model chart, but the concept remains the same. The explanation of the growth stages on the chart is a summary of my understanding of how people develop and grow.

I am deeply grateful to Pastor Steve Overman, senior pastor of Eugene Faith Center and my pastor, for giving me the platform to teach classes using this material for the past four years in the church. Without his support and his encouragement to develop a curriculum to help people develop emotional life skills, this workbook would not have come into being.

I am also grateful to Nancy Carlson, a dear friend for more than 30 years, who designed the cover.

The concept of the "PRAY Process" was developed not to oversimplify the information or because of its easy-to-remember acronym but to give Christians a tool to draw them into the presence of the Lord, where true healing takes place. As with any spiritual tool, used prayerfully and sincerely, it can be helpful in a person's healing. Used to manipulate one's own feelings or those of another person, or employed in a "one-answer-fits-all" approach, it can be hurtful. My prayer is that you will use the concepts in this workbook for healing and growth.

How to Use This Workbook

Personal Growth

Reading through this workbook without doing the exercises will give you a holistic view of health and healing in the Christian life. For some people, this is enough.

Going through the workbook a second time and doing the exercises will add a deeper dimension to your healing and growth process.

Growing Together

Going through the workbook with a friend or a small group of friends can provide an even broader perspective. You can give and receive support, which may help alleviate the "alone" feeling people often have when they are in a healing process.

If you go through this workbook with one or more people, you may want to do the following:

The First Time You Meet

- Become familiar with the format of the workbook.

- Read the preface and Before You Begin together.

- Share with one another what you hope to learn and in what areas you would like to grow.

- Pray together, simply acknowledging God's healing presence.

Week to Week

- Decide on a section of the workbook to do during the week and share your answers to the exercises when you come together again.

    or

- Read the material together in the group and do the exercises together during group time (this will take longer than doing the reading and exercises before you meet). You don't need to go through a set amount of material each week. Go at your own pace.

An hour and a half is a good amount of time to meet as a group. It is helpful to open the time in a short silent or spoken prayer that acknowledges God's presence as the Healer.

During the sharing time, encourage one another to be mindful of all of the group members. Share briefly what you have learned, where you have been touched, and where you need healing. Then move to the next person so everyone who wants to share has time.

It's also very encouraging to look up the verses mentioned throughout this workbook. Many people enjoy incorporating their favorite praise music, poetry, or readings from Psalms (particularly Psalm 23 or Psalm 139) at the end of the group time.

It can be helpful to end the time in silent prayer acknowledging God's healing presence or in spoken prayers mentioning the areas of healing people brought up in the group time.

BEFORE YOU BEGIN

Emotions have gotten a bad rap in church history. Feelings have been misunderstood, aggrandized, denied, mortified, labeled as sin, blamed on the devil—you name it. Understanding, having compassion for, and managing feelings are skills few people develop. These skills are called emotional life skills.

At the core of most dysfunctional behavior lie feelings and needs that have gone unattended. For example, deep feelings of insecurity often lie at the center of a workaholic's frantic behavior. "If I keep working hard," he reasons in an unknown part of himself, "I will have enough to feel more secure and less afraid of *not* having enough in life." In a like vein, the deep need for intimacy often lies at the core of promiscuous behavior. Because needs and feelings can either produce growth or drive us toward dysfunctional behaviors, it makes sense to develop emotional life skills that give us the tools to meet our needs in a healthy manner. One primary emotional life skill we will deal with extensively in this workbook is compassion—the ability to feel empathy for ourselves and others. Learning to live compassionately truly is a road to emotional growth and healing.

Why is it that many Christians don't make it over the long haul? Why do some non-Christians live better, more moral, more fulfilled lives than many Christians? Can a person be spiritually mature without being emotionally mature? What is my part and what is God's part in the journey of the Christian? We will discover answers to these questions as we work through this material together.

My emotional world crumbled many years ago when I was in full-time ministry. I was devastated. My joy turned to depression. I wanted to believe, but I doubted. Anxiety became my constant companion. I did everything I had been taught to do in my discipleship program. It didn't work. It took me years to understand what had happened—years to heal and to change. In the tragedy of September 11, 2001, I recognized an illustration on a global level that helped me understand what sometimes happens to us on an individual level. I was reading a magazine article that stated Osama bin Laden was overjoyed at the results of the crumbling of the twin towers. He had hoped the top floors of the towers would be devastated when the planes flew into them. However, according to this article, he hadn't expected the towers to crumble completely. They crumbled because the inner structures of the buildings were not strong enough to withstand the enormous blast and heat that resulted from the collision.

As we grow up, we develop a "structure" on the inside based on our own temperament and the influence of the environment around us. This structure is not made of steel and is not visible to the eye, but it is real nonetheless. As I grew up, the structure I developed on the inside was full of fear, doubt, and guilt. I was raised with insecurity, lack of emotional safety, and abuse. I compensated by developing certain external skills that allowed me to live successfully for many years. But eventually I was hit with something I couldn't handle, and my interior structure crumbled. I was plunged into a sea of doubt and fear. In the years that followed, I was able to build back an internal structure based on the love of Christ, but it was a slow and arduous process.

My hope is that through what follows you will grow in your understanding of and compassion for yourself and your feelings and in your understanding of your role and God's role in managing those feelings. I pray you will move into a deeper, richer relationship with God, whose love is so unfathomable that few have plumbed its depth. For it is out of this relationship of compassion and love with God that we find ourselves authentically reaching out to meet the needs of other wounded people in our world.

FEELINGS
What's the Big Deal?

I used to not think much about feelings," a friend commented. "I had three feelings: love, anger, and commitment." (He was unaware that commitment is an act of your will and not a feeling.) "Then my wife and I began having problems, and my feelings have gone haywire! I can't get them under control, and they are making me say and do things I don't want to say or do."

What's the big deal about feelings? Feelings tell us about ourselves, others, and the world in which we live. Both pleasant feelings and painful feelings are a part of life. Feelings of love draw us into relationships. Feelings of pain tell us something is wrong. Feelings motivate us to action. Feelings are a part of how God made us.

Yet if we don't understand our feelings, own them, and learn to be wise and gentle in managing and transforming them, they can consciously or unconsciously control us, leading us into behaviors and decisions that are not in our best interest or in the best interest of others. Feelings can rise up and conquer all our good intentions, leading us to make choices even against our values. That's why feelings are a big deal.

When Christians come into a counseling situation, they often 1) feel guilty about focusing on themselves, 2) want to know how they should think about their feelings and especially whether there's a "biblical" way to think about them, and 3) want to know how they can change and grow.

Focusing on Self—A Sin?

To address people's guilt about focusing on themselves, let's look briefly at what we might think of as the "forgotten commandment." One day the Pharisees tested Jesus by posing the question, "Teacher, which is the great commandment in the law?" Jesus answered, "You shall love the Lord your God with all your heart, with all your soul, and with all your mind. This is the first and great commandment. And the second is like it: You shall love your neighbor as yourself" (Matthew 22:36-40). He said that all the rest of the law rested on these commandments: loving God and loving our neighbor as we love ourselves. As believers we talk a lot about loving God and loving others. But we seem to have forgotten the part about loving ourselves. For many Christians the word "self" brings up thoughts of sin, selfishness, badness, and egocentricity. Yet when any aspect of this commandment is being neglected, we are in trouble. We can't truly love others unless we love ourselves. And we don't love ourselves very well until we have been loved by God and have responded in love to Him. Loving God, self, and others is fully intertwined. It's about relationship. There is no love, no life, no healing apart from relationship. We are wounded in relationship, and we will be healed in relationship. Relationship is a spiritual activity.

Day in and day out, countless Christians, at the very least, feel contempt for themselves and, at the very most, hate themselves. Many even feel that the contempt they have for self is a virtue. They mistake contempt for humility. It can take years of self-discovery for these precious people to turn from loathing themselves to loving themselves. It can take years for them to learn to rest in the knowledge that although they are deeply fallen, they are greatly loved.

Talking about our feelings and about loving ourselves, which means having compassion for ourselves, is not a bad thing. It is an integral part of God's most important command.

Thoughts About Feelings

Is there a "biblical" way to think about our feelings? Here are seven misconceptions I have heard over and over again in counseling people toward a more compassionate approach to their feelings.

Common Misconceptions About Feelings

1. "Good" feelings mean I am trusting the Lord while "bad" feelings mean I am not trusting the Lord.

2. Painful feelings are "bad" and may even be sinful.

3. Being filled with the Spirit means I'll only feel good or pleasant feelings.

4. Feelings are a necessary evil.

5. Feelings are unreasonable while logic is reasonable.

6. Feelings should always be subservient to logic.

7. You can never trust your feelings.

A Helpful System of Beliefs About Feelings

Over the years as I've met with countless troubled Christians, I've come to realize that a helpful system of beliefs about their feelings can alleviate a tremendous amount of guilt and suffering. Here are six beliefs that have helped many people as they ask the question, "Is there a biblical way to think about feelings?"

1. Feelings are an aspect of God's likeness in us (Genesis 1-3). For example, God loves, God hates, Jesus wept (sadness), and the Holy Spirit grieves. The fruit of Spirit—love, joy, peace, and the rest—encompasses words that express feelings as well as reveal character qualities.

2. Feelings are not good or bad—they just *are.* If we act on them in destructive ways, they can be harmful.

3. Feelings give us information about ourselves and the world in which we live. They tell us what matters to us or what needs to change.

4. Feelings such as compassion or anger move us to action (Matthew 9:36; Luke 15:20).

5. Feelings connect us to others (Colossians 3:14; Ephesians 3:17; John 4:16).

6. Feelings, repressed, can be destructive. To have repressed feelings means that we are out of touch with what we feel. Psalm 17:10 notes: "They have closed their unfeeling

heart, with their mouth they speak proudly"(NASB),
while Ephesians 4:19 observes: "Feeling no pain, they let
themselves go in sexual obsession, addicted to every sort of
perversion" (MSG).

Over time as we begin to think about our feelings in a less restrictive way and develop a more compassionate approach toward them, our ability to self-regulate our emotions in a healthy manner will increase.

How People Grow

When people are in pain, they ask, "What do I do?" "How can I fix it?" "How do I grow and change?" Unfortunately, they usually don't like the answer. They mistakenly think that if they can get the right information and apply it, they will change quickly. They see change as a mechanical process—a tune-up of sorts. But true transformation, true growth and change, is not an easy or quick process and requires more than a tune-up. It is organic rather than mechanical. It's more like creating a garden. True transformation involves cultivating self-awareness, cultivating the renewal of the mind, and cultivating a healthy environment in which the soul can prosper.

Cultivate Self-Awareness

"I'm not an angry person," a client claims. "I don't know why my coworkers, my wife, and my kids think I need counseling for this. I may get frustrated at times, but I really don't have an anger problem."

"The only time I yell at my kids is when they don't do what I want them to do," a woman laments. "I really am quite a calm person. When others provoke me, I can get a little crazy, but, hey, who doesn't? I don't see why my family wants me to come to counseling."

In both of these examples, the people coming for counseling lack an emotional skill that is vital if they are to grow and change: *self-awareness*. Self-awareness is the ability to know what is going on inside ("What do I think?" "What do I feel?" "Where am I strong?" "Where am I weak?") and to see how we relate to others ("Is my behavior kind and generous?" "Is it abrupt and harsh?" "Am I defensive?" "Am I open to input about myself?"). The more self-awareness a person possesses, the more likely he or she is to grow and to have healthy, meaningful relationships. The psalmist cries out, "Search me, O God, and know my heart; try me and know my anxious thoughts; and see if there be any hurtful way in me, and lead me in the everlasting way" (Psalm 139:23-34). This is a cry for self-awareness and growth! The psalmist also claims that it is God who makes us "know wisdom in [our] innermost being" (Psalm 56:10).

While focusing on knowing oneself is seen as a selfish act in many Christian circles today, many pillars of the faith in generations past knew that knowledge of God and knowledge of self were intricately related.

> Saint Augustine said, "I want to know God and the soul." This was his summary in the opening prayer of his soliloquies.
>
> John Calvin claimed, "True and sound wisdom consists of two parts: the knowledge of God and of ourselves." He introduced this concept of "double knowledge" and wrote about it in *The Institutes of the Christian Religion*.
>
> Soren Kierkegaard reflected, "The more conception of God, the more self: the more self, the more conception of God."
>
> Henri Nouwen suggested, "You cannot know God if you don't even know who you are."
>
> Thomas Merton likened the spiritual life to "a journey in which we discover ourselves in discovering God, and discover God in discovering our true self hidden in God."

So, how do we begin to know ourselves? The Johari Window is a concept developed by two psychologists, Joseph Luft and Harry Ingham. It has been used widely since 1955 to help people better understand their interpersonal communication and relationships. It can be a helpful tool in knowing ourselves.

The Johari Window describes four parts of the self that we all have: the open self, the hidden self, the blind self, and the unknown self.

	What we know about ourselves	What we don't know about ourselves
What others know about us	Open Self 1	Blind Self 3
What others don't know about us	Hidden Self 2	Unknown Self 4

Johari Window

The *open self* (1) is the part of us that contains the things we know about ourselves and others know about us. "I hate coconut, and everyone who knows me knows I hate coconut!" or "I consider myself a kind person, and most people who know me would say that I am kind."

The *hidden self* (2) is the part of us that contains things we know about ourselves but don't let other people see. "I don't like myself very much, but others wouldn't know that because I come across as confident," or "People see me as a strong Christian because I know the talk, but I don't let them see how much doubt I have inside."

The *blind self* (3) is the part of us that contains things others know about us but we don't know about ourselves. "I see myself as a person who is on time regularly, but my friends have begun to tell me how frustrated they are with me because I frequently run late," or "I see myself as easy-going, but the people who are the closest to me have begun to tell me they think I am controlling."

The *unknown self* (4) is the part of us that is beyond our awareness and unseen by others. We are complex, and even the most self-aware people have deep places within themselves that are out of reach to their conscious minds. Other people don't see these places within us either. Only God knows this part of us fully (Psalm 139).

The study questions at the end of the chapter (especially question number 3) will help you get to know yourself better. Taking time to get know yourself is an important part of the Christian life. Knowing yourself helps you to bring all of who you are into your relationship with God, where true healing takes place.

Cultivate the Renewing of Your Mind

In Romans 12:1-2 Paul admonishes us to renew our minds. In my early Christian training, this meant memorizing Scripture and using it to counter any unscriptural thoughts. Although this was and is a productive spiritual discipline, there is more to renewing our minds than this one practice.

Renewing our minds involves both our thinking *and* our feelings. Both thoughts and feelings originate in the brain. When Paul talked about renewing our minds, he was talking about renewing both our thoughts and our feelings. The feeling part of the brain develops first and contains every feeling we've ever had, both pleasant and painful. When feelings become too painful, we can repress them. They can go into hiding but come back to bite us when triggered by a present circumstance. The thinking part of the brain develops later, and as we grow we learn how to think about and interpret our feelings. The thinking brain has many components, including the capacity to learn, to solve problems, and to evaluate what we know and feel. However, what we consciously know in our "thinking brain" is a fraction of what is contained in our "feeling brain." This means we can sometimes have feelings and not know where they are coming from. Or we can "know" that we are loved but "feel" as if we are not loved.

To renew our minds, then, involves both our feelings and our thinking. Renewing our thinking requires truth (knowledge). Renewing our feelings requires love (experience). A.W. Tozier, in his book *Knowledge of the Holy,* says that "faith is the organ of knowledge and love is the organ of experience." Paul says that what is important is "faith working through love" (Galatians 5). So truth (knowledge/faith) combined with love (experience) is what is needed to renew our minds.

To illustrate this, consider people who never know love growing up. They come to faith in Christ, but they struggle to believe God loves them. They can memorize Scriptures about God's love until the cows come home but not *feel* God's love. They are attempting to renew only the thinking part of the brain. Now if along with this practice they get involved in a safe, loving community and begin to *feel* loved, their experience will begin to transform the feeling brain. Both are essential. This process is not quick. It takes time.

Cultivate a Healthy Environment for Your Soul to Prosper

Nature is a beautiful teacher. Embedded in the cells of every plant is a blueprint for growth. Given the right soil and the right amount of sunshine and water, any plant will grow. The human soul is the same. In our very cells, we are wired to grow. But how well we grow and heal depends on the "soil" in which we are planted. In the book *Changes That Heal,* Henry Cloud suggests that since the fall (Genesis 3), three elements have been necessary for the healing of human nature: *grace, truth,* and *time.*

Grace. Grace is God's attitude toward us at all times. It is God's unmerited favor and love that cannot be thwarted. Cloud suggests that grace is love expressing itself to us not as an idea but as a real relationship of favor. Love invites us out of isolation and into relationship where we can be healed.

Truth. We need direction and limits in life to keep us from falling into old patterns or from fooling ourselves about attitudes and behaviors that cause hurt and pain. Truth provides this by helping us discern good from evil and know right from wrong (Hebrews 5:14). Truth is embodied in Jesus Christ. The Bible tells us that the Holy Spirit will lead us into all truth (John 16:13).

Jesus Christ is the embodiment of *both* grace and truth (John 1:14-18). Unfortunately people tend to split into two separate camps regarding grace and truth. In one camp are those who think talking too much about grace gives people a license to sin. In the other camp are those who think talking too much about truth leads to rigid dogmatism. In reality, grace without truth leads to *license*, while truth without grace leads to *judgment*. Holding grace and truth together, however, keeps us from falling into either of these two faulty ways of thinking.

When people feel truly known and accepted in a relationship, it provides an environment of safety. God loves us completely and knows us intimately. That is fertile soil!

Time. As we look at Scripture, we see that time is an essential ingredient of growth. In passages such as 1 Peter 3:18, Hebrews 5:8, and Luke 2:52 (and many more), we see that growth and maturity involve a process. Often we want instant healing or growth. Taking shortcuts is a constant temptation (for instance, promiscuity is easier than the difficult work of emotional intimacy).

Mark 4:26-29 reveals an important truth about the growth process. The kingdom of God is like a seed you plant. You go to sleep, and when you wake up, the seed has grown into a plant. Its growth cannot be willed or controlled. The same is true about emotional growth. It can be cultivated and enhanced only as you plant yourself in relationships of grace and truth and give that environment time to work. If you are depressed, it does you no good to try to be "undepressed." You need to get into loving relationships, be open to truth, and give these elements time. In other words, you need to change the focus from the symptoms (depression, rage, addictions) to the responsible cultivation of the soil.

Many people ask me about growth and prayer. Just as we go through physical stages as we mature from childhood to adulthood, we also go through emotional stages. The physical stages are easy to see. The emotional stages are not as discernable because they happen inside of us. As a young child of 6 or 7, I remember wanting to be older. I wanted to be 16 so I could drive. I wanted to be 18 so I could be an adult. If I had prayed that I would hurry up and be 16 or 18 and had expected that to happen instantly, or if I had asked God to make the years go faster, I would have been sorely disappointed. God has placed a natural growth sequence in our cells, and we grow according to that. No matter how much I had prayed or wanted to be older, I would have had to wait to grow through all the stages of development.

In the same way, a natural emotional growth process is programmed into our very cells (more about this in chapter 2). If I am 10 years old emotionally and want to be as emotionally mature as a 21-year-old, I doubt that will happen—no matter how much I pray about it. I have to grow through the natural stages of emotional development. If I get wounded in a particular emotional stage, a part of my emotional growth can get "stuck" at that age. To pray for that part of me to instantly grow from feeling like a wounded 10-year-old to feeling like a healed 20-, 30-, or

40-year-old is unrealistic. I have to go back and deal with those stages. However, when we go back as adults to heal and grow through the stages where we became stuck, it doesn't take as long as it originally would have because not every part of us is stuck at that stage. Prayer is a way to allow God to walk with us in our healing and growth, giving us strength and courage to keep going when we don't think we can go another day. It is rarely a path to an instant healing of our wounds.

GOING DEEPER:
Getting to Know Yourself

1. Explain how you have viewed your feelings in the past. (Were they good or bad, right or wrong, something to be ignored, something to be given into, or something else?)

2. Reread the sections "Common Misconceptions About Feelings" and "A Helpful System of Beliefs About Feelings." Which do you identify with and why?

3. Go to Appendix A, the Johari Window: Getting to Know Yourself, and use it as an individual exercise or as group exercise. How was the exercise on self-awareness helpful? On a scale from 1 to 10, 1 being "I don't know myself well" and 10 being "I know myself very well," where would you rate yourself and why?

4. After reading this chapter, what has changed in your thinking about feelings?

5. What are ways you can create a safe environment of "grace, truth, and time" in which to grow?

6. Go to Appendix B, the Feelings Log, and use it every day for a week as an individual exercise. You can copy the chart for further use.

A BIBLICAL GROWTH MODEL

*"I would never want to be a Christian. They talk a good
talk but rarely live it. At least I'm not a hypocrite."*

*"How come some non-Christians I know
live better lives than Christians?"*

*"I don't understand what God's part is and
what my part is in the Christian life."*

often hear these comments, and many like them, in my office. In this chapter, I want to address concerns such as these by offering a model of growth that combines a biblical perspective with a developmental approach to human nature. The chart on pages 26-27, A Biblical Growth Model, will help you as you search for a clearer understanding of the Christian life. It is, of course, limited by the fact that it is one-dimensional. It is difficult to show on a chart the depth and fluid motion of human growth. Also, rarely is human growth as symmetrical as the chart indicates. However, the chart does show how people can move toward a relationship with Christ based on love and freedom and not guilt and fear. If it seems too technical, please feel free to skip this chapter. You will still be able to discover and learn to develop emotional life skills necessary for effective living.

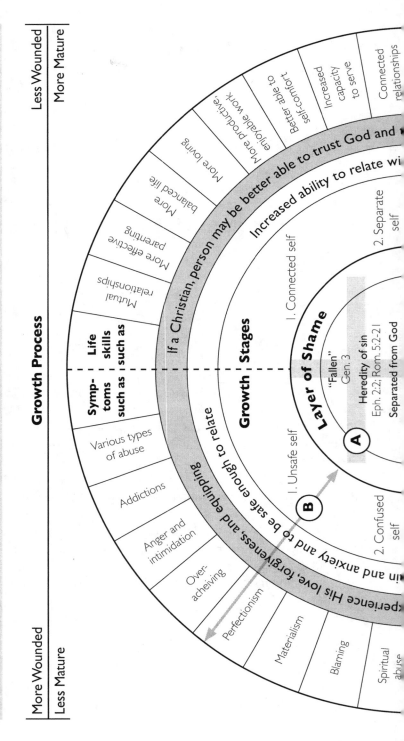

A BIBLICAL GROWTH MODEL

2 Peter 3:18

More Wounded	Less Wounded
Less Mature	More Mature

Growth Process

Increased ability to relate with...

If a Christian, person may be better able to trust God and...

...experience His love, forgiveness and to be safe enough to relate

...in and anxiety and to be safe enough to relate

Symptoms such as
- Various types of abuse
- Addictions
- Anger and intimidation
- Over-achieving
- Perfectionism
- Materialism
- Blaming
- Spiritual abuse

Life skills such as
- Mutual relationships
- More effective parenting
- More balanced life
- More loving
- More productive, enjoyable work
- Better able to self-comfort
- Increased capacity to serve
- Connected relationships

Growth Stages

1. Connected self
2. Separate self

1. Unsafe self
2. Confused self

A

Layer of Shame

"Fallen" Gen. 3

Heredity of sin
Eph. 2:2; Rom. 5:2-21

Separated from God

B

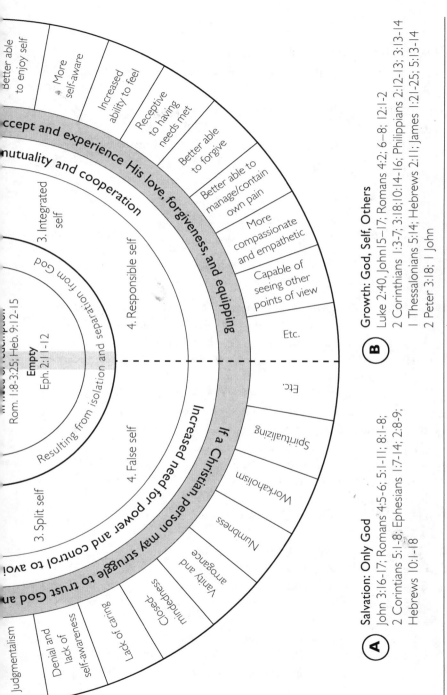

Better able to enjoy self

More self-aware

Increased ability to feel

Receptive to having needs met

Better able to forgive

Better able to manage/contain own pain

More compassionate and empathetic

Capable of seeing other points of view

Etc.

Accept and experience His love, forgiveness, and equipping

Mutuality and cooperation

3. Integrated self

Drawing from God

4. Responsible self

Empty
Eph. 2:11-12

...Need of Redemption
Rom. 1:8-3:25; Heb. 9:12-15

Resulting from isolation and separation from God

3. Split self

4. False self

Increased need for power and control to avoid...

If a Christian, person may struggle to trust God and...

Etc.

Etc.

Spiritualizing

Workaholism

Numbness

Vanity and arrogance

Closed-mindedness

Lack of caring

Denial and lack of self-awareness

Judgmentalism

(A) Salvation: Only God

John 3:16-17; Romans 4:5-6; 5:1-11; 8:1-8;
2 Corinthians 5:1-8; Ephesians 1:7-14; 2:8-9;
Hebrews 10:1-18

(B) Growth: God, Self, Others

Luke 2:40, John15-17; Romans 4:2; 6-8; 12:1-2
2 Corinthians 1:3-7; 3:18;10:14-16; Philippians 2:12-13; 3:13-14
I Thessalonians 5:14; Hebrews 2:11; James 1:21-25; 5:13-14
2 Peter 3:18; I John

HUDSON/REXIUS © 2006

A Biblical Growth Model Explained

We are continually in a growth process in life. Rarely are we stagnant. As represented by the line across the top of the Growth Model, we are moving from a more wounded, less mature space in life toward a less wounded, more mature space in life. This isn't always a smooth process and there can be starts and stops, but if we want to grow and if we stay in healthy relationships (we were wounded in relationships; we'll be healed in relationships), we can't help but grow and heal.

More Wounded	**Growth Process**	Less Wounded
Less Mature		More Mature

Center Circle

Before the fall recorded in Genesis 3, Adam and Eve lived in communion with God and with each other without sin, shame, fear, or aloneness. They were "naked and unashamed." At their very core, or soul, they were whole, and they made sense to themselves and to each other. Their need for relationship was met. They belonged. All was "good."

Adam and Eve sinned by trusting themselves and withdrawing from communion with God. In thinking they knew more than God, they plunged themselves and the rest of the human race into isolation and separation from God. Separated from God, they didn't make sense to themselves or to each other. Where before they were other-centered, they now found themselves self-centered. Where before they felt connected, they now felt empty and alone. Where they were once vulnerable and safe, they now were vulnerable and ashamed. Out of fear they hid from God. Ever since then every person has been born into the world *greatly loved and valued,* *yet deeply fallen and in need of redemption.* As a result of this separation and isolation from God, a layer of shame covers every human heart.

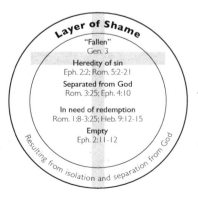

Layer of Shame

"Fallen"
Gen. 3

Heredity of sin
Eph. 2:2; Rom. 5:2-21

Separated from God
Rom. 3:25; Eph. 4:10

In need of redemption
Rom. 1:8-3:25; Heb. 9:12-15

Empty
Eph. 2:11-12

Resulting from isolation and separation from God

Only God, through salvation, can touch that deep place within us. By becoming a man in the person of His Son, Jesus Christ, and entering our sin-stained world, God provided a way for us to end our isolation and separation from Him. Christ, through His death and resurrection, dealt with sin once and for all. When we trust in Jesus to free us from this condition, we no longer remain separated from God and our redemption is sealed. Jesus begins to soak up the layer of shame covering our hearts.

Growth Stages

Every person goes through growth stages both physically and emotionally. The physical growth stages are easy to identify, but the emotional stages of growth may be more subtle and less easily understood as we grow into adulthood. Ideally, parents provide an environment for children to move through the emotional growth stages. Children don't need "perfect" parents. They need "good enough" parents who are loving, who parent with compassion and appropriate direction, and who own their mistakes. If, because of a lack of proper parenting or other external problems, we don't move through the emotional process of growth, we can "get stuck" in certain stages. That's when we become symptomatic; that is, we feel depressed or anxious, we don't manage our feelings well, or we feel like a child in an adult's body.

A brief and very limited view of the stages of growth may be helpful.

1. Unsafe Self Versus Connected Self

We can't live in isolation. When a baby is born, he immediately seeks emotional connection. This process is where he learns to trust. If a baby bonds with adults in his life, and they are safe, giving, emotionally mature people, the baby learns that his needs will be met, and the *feeling* that he is safe, that people can be trusted, and that he belongs begins to grow inside of the child. A child is not automatically born with these feelings. If a child is delighted in, if he is celebrated, and if his needs are met, he learns to rest and trust, knowing his well-being is being guarded by those who love him. This allows a child to begin to develop a "self" inside that is comfortable connecting with others (the *connected self*). In that connection he gets his emotional needs met.

If the adults in the baby's life are not safe, are not more interested in meeting his needs than their own, do not provide safety, or are not

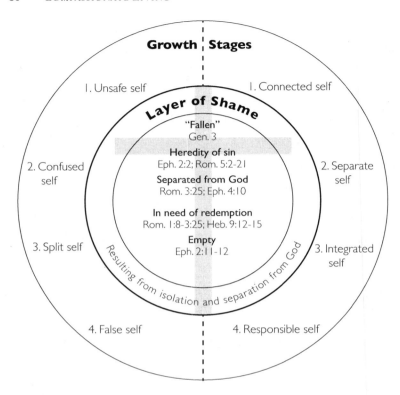

Growth Stages

1. Unsafe self

1. Connected self

Layer of Shame

"Fallen"
Gen. 3

Heredity of sin
Eph. 2:2; Rom. 5:2-21

Separated from God
Rom. 3:25; Eph. 4:10

In need of redemption
Rom. 1:8-3:25; Heb. 9:12-15

Empty
Eph. 2:11-12

2. Confused self

2. Separate self

3. Split self

3. Integrated self

Resulting from isolation and separation from God

4. False self

4. Responsible self

consistent in their love and attention toward the child, the child cannot connect in a way that allows him to trust and take in a feeling that he is safe. He can't trust the connection and therefore doesn't take in a deep sense of belonging. He develops a "self" inside that feels unsafe connecting (the *unsafe self*), and it becomes difficult to get his needs met.

This stage extends from the womb to about three years old. However, connecting is a skill that is necessary throughout life. In fact, each of these stages has a fairly predictable age range, give or take a few years, but the skills learned in each of these stages must be negotiated throughout the lifespan.

It goes without saying that *any* form of child abuse during this stage or any of the stages is extremely damaging and can hinder the development of emotional skills in a child. *Spiritual abuse* occurs when the adults in a child's life inappropriately use the Bible and God to shame, guilt, or frighten a child into conforming. *Emotional and psychological abuse* occurs when adults intentionally or unintentionally use techniques such as coercion, fear, manipulation, shame, and guilt to get a child to do what they want him to do. In *verbal abuse,* parents use words, tone of voice, or volume of voice to make a child get in line (yelling, belittling, name calling). *Physical abuse* occurs when adults use physical force to get a child to conform (hitting with a belt or stick, slapping, shoving). *Sexual abuse* can range from an atmosphere in which adults regularly use inappropriate sexual language and innuendoes around the child to introducing the child to pornography, sexually touching the child or having the child sexually touch them, or sexual intercourse. When child abuse happens in any form, it disrupts the stages of growth and hinders a child from forming a healthy sense of self on the inside. Instead, the child is riddled with feelings ranging from depression and anxiety to extreme forms of self-hate, rejection, rage, and terror.

2. Confused Self Versus Separate Self

As a child feels secure in her connection with others, she begins to move toward having a *separate self.* The child begins to recognize that there are boundaries between her and others. She begins to explore—to risk being on her own—while all the time keeping an eye on mom or another nurturing adult in her life. If the child is encouraged in this process, with mom and dad providing lots of love and appropriate limits while not doing for the child what she can do for herself or overwhelming her by not giving enough support, the child develops a feeling of self-confidence on the inside. She develops a feeling that she is competent, can create, and can accomplish tasks. She begins to develop a sense of confidence as she relates to other children.

If the adults in the child's life are too rigid or frightened and restrict the child too much, she develops a feeling of fear on the inside. She doesn't learn to have self-confidence but looks to others for direction and approval. If the adults in her life are punitive or shaming when she ventures out (naturally making mistakes), she begins to feel guilt and shame on the inside about who she is and what she does. She is left with a sense on the inside of confusion (the *confused self*). Being confused on the inside results in a lack of confidence in relating to others or in accomplishing tasks.

This stage normally occurs from about three years of age to about nine through eleven. Having a separate identity and the ability to connect with others is the basis for true intimacy in adulthood.

3. Split Self Versus Integrated Self

As children grow through the difficult and often turbulent adolescent years, one of their tasks is to figure out who they are in relationship to others. Peers play a critical role in this period of development. If adolescents have a sense of belonging and are somewhat self-confident (this stage really challenges self-confidence), they begin to see themselves and others realistically. They begin to develop another emotional skill, that of seeing people and circumstances as not "all good" or "all bad." They begin to see that the world is not all black or all white. During this stage adolescents begin to know, and to come to terms with, their strengths and weaknesses. They have no need to reject their less-than-perfect selves because they know that everyone shares in this human condition. Consequently they learn to take responsibility for their choices and all the consequences of their choices without guilt or self-condemnation. They begin to develop an *integrated self,* where who they are on the inside is who they are on the outside.

If adolescents don't enter this period with a sense of belonging and if they lack in self-confidence, this stage can be excruciating. If parents and other adults in their lives are punitive, too rigid, too shaming, too lenient, not understanding, or the like, adolescents have no choice but to judge their less-than-perfect self (their weaknesses) and begin developing a *split self.* They feel "all good" when they meet the standards of their peers or adults around them, but they feel "all bad" when they don't meet those standards. They don't learn how to accept the good and bad in themselves or in others. Everything begins to be seen as black or white. They aren't able to explore their strengths and weaknesses because this threatens their inner world too much. They have difficulty taking responsibility for their choices because any mistake or error triggers shame, guilt, and "I'm less than" feelings. So they hide their true self and begin to develop a false self. Being critical and judgmental is a characteristic of a person caught in this stage, as is rebelling and becoming an "all bad" person to hide the deeper feelings of inadequacy.

This stage lasts throughout adolescence and continues through young adulthood.

4. False Self Versus Responsible Self

As young people grow through these stages into adulthood, they grow into the *responsible self.* They have a sense of belonging and a relatively good sense of self-confidence. They know themselves—with their strengths, weaknesses, and ability to make choices—and are comfortable in their own skins. They are relatively integrated selves—they're real on the inside and the outside. They know how to meet their own needs, and yet they can delay gratification if the time or place is not appropriate. They don't need to be in "one up/one down" relationships. That is, they don't need to take an "I'm in control" stance. Neither do they crumble and take a "one down" position with others, an "I need to be taken care of" stance. Mutual relationships are much more satisfying. These people have a sense of wanting to give to the next generation, and they find themselves serving their family, friends, and community.

People who have not negotiated the first three growth stages reach adulthood with a *false self.* They either don't know or are hiding their true, less-than-perfect self and have developed a false self that relates to the world. This false self may look good on the outside, but inside lies a person who feels inadequate, confused, angry, and frightened. As a result, maintaining this false self takes all their energy. If their false self is ever seen for what it is, they may react by showing their anger, denying their faults, or taking the "one up/one down" position in relationship to others. It takes all of their energy to maintain this dance within themselves and with others, and so they remain lonely, self-absorbed, depressed, anxious, and unable to engage in mutually satisfying relationships. They don't know how to meet their needs and secretly think others should do this for them. They may give to their family and friends and try to serve the next generation, but their motive is self-serving—they want to feel good about themselves. It is not the overflow of a generous heart.

This stage extends from young adulthood through the rest of life.

It is important to understand that no one falls completely on one side or the other of the growth stages. People fall somewhere between the two extremes because no one has had perfect parenting or been unaffected by life circumstances.

Three Outside Rings

If a person's journey through the growth stages falls more on the left side of the chart, he develops an increased need for power and control in order to avoid pain and anxiety and in order to be feel safe enough to relate to others. This is true for believers and nonbelievers alike. Becoming a Christian does not automatically heal all the emotional damage we have experienced in life, nor does it resolve the stages of growth we haven't been able to negotiate and in which we have therefore become stuck. After the first freeing experience of becoming a Christian (recognizing that God has done for us what we couldn't do for ourselves in providing our salvation) fades, the growth process (sanctification) begins. This is where Christians who were raised in ways resulting in the characteristics on the left side of the chart find themselves struggling to trust God and experience His love, forgiveness, and equipping. The symptoms seen on the outer circle follow.

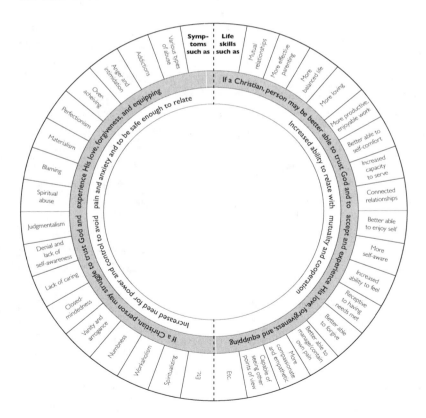

Let me offer a word of encouragement here for those who struggle with emotional damage from their background. I have heard doctors say that when a bone is broken and reset, it is stronger after it heals than before it was broken. This can also be true with emotional healing. As you grow through the "dark night of the soul" of the healing process, you will truly find that God is near to the brokenhearted, and you will become, as Henri Nouwen suggests, one of the wounded healers of the world.

People who have been fortunate enough to fall more on the right side of the chart in their growth stages have less to overcome and have an increased ability to relate to others with mutuality and cooperation. The result is that they are more equipped with emotional skills that make life pleasant and fulfilling. This is true of believers and nonbelievers. This is why nonbelievers sometimes appear to live better lives than Christians. They may not be "saved," but they have greater emotional skills with which to handle life. When these nonbelievers become Christians, they are better able to *feel* trusting of God and have a greater ability to experience God's love, forgiveness, and equipping. The life skills on the outer circle on the right side of the chart follow. These people are ones to whom the admonition "to you who have been given much, shall much be required" (Luke 12:48) might apply.

Anyone whose background lies more to the left side of the chart may feel "That's not fair!" No, it's not fair. And it leads to the theological and deeply emotional issues of suffering and evil in this world. While it is not the scope of this workbook to address these issues, scores of excellent books on these topics are available. I do know that God has not left us alone, nor has He left us without resources. He walks with us in and through every painful experience we have in life. As we plant ourselves in the fertile soil of grace and truth and give the process time, we can't help but see the fruit of healing in our lives.

God's Part and My Part

Turn back to pages 26-27 and look again at A Biblical Growth Model. Perhaps now the whole chart looks less daunting, and we can attempt to answer the question, "What's God part and what's my part in the Christian life?" Find the letter "A" on the cross in the center circle. That represents salvation. I believe salvation is completely God's part. It's not up to me.

It's His job, and I can rest in His provision. Take a look at the corresponding letter "A" on the lower left-hand side of the chart that says, "Salvation: Only God." As you look up the verses mentioned there, you will find that you can completely relax in God's overwhelming provision.

Now look at the letter "B" that extends from the center circle to the outside layer on the left side of the chart. This represents growth (change, sanctification, transformation). This is where you come in. This part of the process requires a loving relationship with God, with yourself, and with others. It is something that God partners in with you, and you with Him, in the community of His people. Look at the corresponding letter "B" on the lower right-hand side of the chart that says, "Growth: God, Self, Others." Look up the verses to gain insight into this lifelong process.

Note: When I say God partners with us, I'm talking about fellowship with the triune God: Father, Son, and Holy Spirit. The Holy Spirit dwells within believers, giving strength and healing from the inside out. The triune God is everywhere, working from the outside in. In the fellowship of the Father, the Son, and Holy Spirit, surrounded by the community of believers, there is hope beyond measure. With the apostle Paul, our hearts lift in prayer: "I ask—ask the God of our Master, Jesus Christ, the God of glory—to make you intelligent and discerning in knowing Him personally, your eyes focused and clear, so that you can see exactly what it is He is calling you to do, grasp the immensity of this glorious way of life He has for Christians, oh, the utter extravagance of His work in us who trust Him—endless energy, boundless strength!" (Ephesians 1:17-19 MSG).

A Word About Needs

We all have needs. We have a need to be secure, a need to belong, a need to be loved, a need to be significant, a need to be valued, a need to be accomplished, and many more. Having needs is a normal part of our human condition and is what draws us into relationship with God and others.

When we are children, these needs are what we might call "Big *N*" needs. Babies are utterly dependent on the adults in their lives to meet these needs and to give them a sense that they are secure, that they belong, and that they are loved. They don't automatically have these feelings inside of them.

As children grow up in a healthy environment where their needs are valued and met, the desperateness they feel to have the adults in their lives meet these needs becomes less and less. This is because on the *inside* they are feeling more secure, more like they belong, and more like they are valuable. This is a gradual process.

By the time children reach adulthood, these needs, though still present, have become what we might call "little *n*" needs. People still need (little *n*) to be loved, but they are not utterly dependent on others to make that happen. They feel loved inside and know how to reach out to get their need to be loved met in healthy relationships.

Many people do not grow into adults having had their Big *N* needs met in childhood. So they unknowingly bring their Big *N* needs into their adult relationships. It is not that they need (little *n*) to be loved, but they desperately need (Big *N*) the other person to love them or they don't feel loved on the inside. Bringing our Big *N* needs into our adult relationships may feel good at first because we finally feel we are getting what we didn't get as children. However, eventually it will wear that relationship out. Often in relationships both people bring their Big *N* needs into the relationship. One or the other person will have to get away from that kind of demand or burn out. These Big *N* needs can be resolved through avenues such as counseling, grieving, involvement in community, and building relationship with God, but no single person can meet these needs. They cannot be met in the exact same way as a child's needs can be met because we are now adults.

The Place of Forgiveness

Earnest Christians come into my office daily with questions about the part forgiveness plays in the healing process: "My Bible study leader told me that I haven't forgiven my father for belittling me as a kid and that's why I'm still struggling with bad feelings about him. Is that true?" "I feel so guilty because I keep trying to forgive my wife for the affair she had, but my anger and hurt keep coming back. What's wrong?" "I don't want to forgive the drunk driver who smashed into our car! It feels like I'm letting him off the hook." People with questions and feelings like these have often been taught that forgiveness is the one and only answer to many of their debilitating feelings toward people who have hurt them. They tell stories about well-meaning counselors who, on hearing their stories, ask immediately, "Have you forgiven them?" when those coming for counsel haven't even fully "felt" the offenses against them yet, let alone forgiven the people responsible for those offenses.

Although forgiveness is not the focus of this workbook, it is a central theme in the Bible. Forgiving yourself and forgiving others is a practice that leads to healthy living. A popular saying goes: "To not forgive someone is like swallowing poison and waiting for the other person to die." Forgiveness is important. However, forgiveness is only one part of the healing process (see "Overview of the Healing Process" [Appendix C]).

Over the years I have come to believe that forgiveness is both a choice in time and a process. With our wills we can choose to align ourselves with God and ask Him for the ability to forgive someone at a moment in time. However, the ability to *feel* forgiveness usually requires a process that involves feeling the hurt, anger, and grief over the offense before we can feel the forgiveness.

A word of caution here. Sometimes we use forgiveness as a way to avoid or manipulate feelings—our own or someone else's. It goes like this: I do something wrong or unkind, and I feel bad about myself. I ask you to forgive me, but what I really want is to feel better. I want you to not feel bad about what I did because that makes me feel bad about me. So I want you to hurry up and forgive me. I don't even give you time to process the event. The same thing can happen in reverse if someone hurts me.

You need to give people space and time to forgive. Let me give a scenario that, though extreme, may help illustrate what I'm saying. Let's say I am stepping into a crosswalk with a green light. A person in a car accidently runs a red light and hits me. I'm rushed to the hospital with a broken leg and hip. After surgery I am in the ICU and have been told that I will need many months of painful physical therapy in order to be able to use my leg again. The man who hit me comes to see me in the ICU and through his tears asks me to forgive him. I genuinely do. Furthermore he is so sorry for what he did that he comes almost every day to support me during my physical therapy sessions. Now, imagine the following. I'm grimacing with pain as I'm taking a few steps, and he looks at me and says, "I thought you forgave me? Every time you show me your pain, it makes me feel bad. It makes me think you haven't forgiven me." Foolish, isn't it? Yet that's how we tend to think about forgiveness when it comes to our emotions. If you forgive, you won't have any painful feelings about the experience. That's just not true.

Another Dimension—Spiritual Warfare

The scope of this workbook does not include the many facets of spiritual warfare. You may need to talk with someone you trust who is knowledgeable about this topic or who can recommend books for you to read. Spiritual warfare is a fact in the Christian life. We have a very real foe who would love nothing better than to see us destroyed. Yet my caution about spiritual warfare is that often *all* painful feelings are blamed on the devil. Some people claim there are "demons" of depression, lust, fear, and the like. They reason that when they get rid of these demons, the painful feelings will go away. This can lead to various unhealthy attitudes toward feelings. One attitude is that because these feelings are demons, people are not responsible for them. The goal becomes getting the demons "cast out" rather than pursuing emotional health and healing, which takes time and perseverance. Another attitude is that healing of painful feelings can be an event that happens instantly or perhaps with a few casting-out sessions. Both of these approaches lead to immaturity and can cause deep feelings of guilt and failure when the feelings return.

A healthier approach for people struggling with painful feelings would be to stand firm (Ephesians 6) behind Jesus and ask Him to deal with anything that may be demonic in their suffering. Then, holding His hand, they can begin dealing with the feelings that are troubling them. Jesus doesn't leave us to the wiles of the enemy of our souls during the painful, often dark times of emotional suffering.

GOING DEEPER:
Identifying Areas of Growth and Healing

Refer to the chart "A Biblical Growth Model" on pages 26-27 as you answer these questions.

1. Looking at the continuum across the top of the page, if "More Wounded, Less Mature" is a 1 and "Less Wounded, More Mature" is a 10, how would you rate yourself and why?

2. Look at the four "Growth Stages." Would you say you land more on the left side, on the right side, or somewhere in between? Write a few sentences about your observations.

3. Each growth stage corresponds with an age range: Stage 1, one to about three years old; Stage 2, three to about nine, ten or eleven years old; Stage 3, throughout adolescence and continuing through young adulthood; and Stage 4, a lifetime of growth. Write down both positive and painful memories you have in each of these stages. How do you think you were affected by these events? How do the feelings you have about these events affect your view of God? (Use a journal or a separate piece of paper for this question. Also, this may take a considerable amount of time, so be patient with yourself.)

4. Looking at the outside circle, identify "Symptoms" you may have along the left side of the chart. Identify "Life skills" you may have along the right side of the chart. What do you feel as you identify these traits? Which traits would you like to change or grow in?

5. God is the perfect parent. He is the "father/mother" God. How would your life be different if you could let God reparent you in the areas where you were wounded? Journal about this or talk to a safe, trusted friend.

THE PRAY PROCESS
Managing and Transforming Feelings with Compassion

When people come to the counseling office, they are usually seeking pain reduction. Their internal or external world (or both) is out of control, resulting in a painful emotional crisis. As the crisis moves toward resolution, many of these people choose to move toward a bigger goal: growth and maturity.

As noted in chapter 2, if we as children don't get what we need growing up because of neglect or abuse, we may end up with painful, unexplained feelings in the present. We may also discover that we struggle with basic emotional life skills necessary for healthy living. To grow and mature, we need to address these concerns.

First, let's look at four emotional life skills that can be developed if they have not already been. Then we will delve into the principles undergirding the PRAY Process, a tool that can be used to help develop these four emotional life skills and regulate painful emotions that get triggered in everyday life. Some people may need the additional help of a counselor to deal with deep childhood trauma.

Healing is a lifelong journey. The PRAY Process helps people on this journey. It is meant to help hurting people bring the Lord into the middle of their pain. So often when people hurt, they pull away from God as a result of shame or fear. They judge their feelings. They don't know how to let God, through His Spirit, enter the painful places inside of them to comfort and heal.

Emotional Life Skills

As we grow from childhood to adulthood, we learn skills without even knowing we are doing so. For example, children raised in a bilingual family don't remember learning both languages. They just know both because they learned them together as they matured.

What is true of a cognitive skill such as language acquisition is also true of emotional skills. If we have had "good enough" parenting (no one has had perfect parenting), we naturally develop emotional skills that will carry us through life, though we usually don't remember doing so. Four of these skills are *self-awareness, containment of feelings, self-comfort,* and *empathy.*

If the environment growing up was not conducive to developing these skills, we will need to develop them. Learning these skills as adults is difficult and awkward—much like learning a foreign language. However, if we fail to learn a second language after we reach adulthood, it may not make a significant difference in our quality of life. But if we don't learn emotional skills, the quality of our relationships will suffer tremendously.

Below are definitions of the above four *emotional life skills.*

1. *Self-awareness:* the ability to *observe* what is going on around you and within you in the present moment. It includes the ability to label your feelings and "stay with them" (feel them and not repress them) until you decide what to do with them. It also involves the ability to describe what you see and feel without judgment. Self-aware people know their strengths and weaknesses and are open to growth.

2. *Containment of feelings:* the ability to *hold* or *contain* your feelings within your own boundary lines. An example is feeling angry and being able to talk about it without exploding, yelling, or throwing things. If you do the latter, it is called "spilling over" onto someone else and making them the "container" of your big feelings. Another example would be overreacting to an event (sobbing, screaming, collapsing) and expecting someone else to "fix it" for you.

3. *Self-comfort:* the ability to *soothe* or *nurture* yourself emotionally when painful feelings well up within you. For example, you've had a draining day at work and look forward to going home and talking to your wife about it. You've forgotten she has a school board meeting that evening.

Totally frustrated, you have to decide how to comfort yourself. Positive ways to do so might be to pray, call a friend, go for a run, cook your favorite meal, or read the paper. Negative ways to comfort yourself might include drinking too much, eating too much, feeling sorry for yourself, using pornography, barking at the kids, or being grumpy and taking it out on your wife when she returns home. To develop the skill of self-comfort, you need to take the time to get to know yourself and develop numerous healthy forms of comfort (try to think of a dozen). It's like having a toolbox to choose from when the need arises.

4. *Empathy:* the ability to feel compassion for yourself and others through the painful parts of life (hurts, failures, losses). Empathy also includes the ability to feel joy in life and to share in the joys of others. Compassion, loving-kindness, and mercy are inseparable. Having empathy involves developing an attitude of compassion and curiosity instead of an attitude of condemnation and judgment toward yourself and others.

These life skills can be developed as you grow. The PRAY Process is a tool that encompasses all four of these skills. As you use this process consistently over time, you will learn to regulate and transform your feelings while developing these skills.

The Principles of the PRAY Process

Below is an overview of the four core principles of the PRAY process.

Principle 1: Every person has *core value*.

Principle 2: Because we live in a broken, fallen world, every person has *core hurt*.

Principle 3: As people grow and heal, they can more freely choose to live out of their *core value* and not out of their *core hurt*.

Principle 4: Believers have the indwelling presence of the Holy Spirit to partner with them in choosing to live out of their *core value*.

The concepts of core value and core hurt (and healing the core hurt with compassion) are adapted from the work of Stephen Stosny in *You Don't Have to Take It Anymore.**

Principle 1: Every person has core value.

Core value is something we are born with. Because we are made in the image of God (Genesis 1) we have intrinsic self-worth. Core value and intrinsic self-worth are synonymous. Our feelings and our bodies can be hurt in life. Our core value can feel diminished at times, but it can never be destroyed, because our value is intrinsically God-given. It is from this core value that we find the capacity to care for others and to be cared about by others. The ability to feel or experience our core value comes through compassion—compassion for ourselves and for others (1 John 4:7-21; Matthew 22:36-40; Colossians 3:12; Psalm 103:13). This is why compassion is such an important emotional life skill. It is key in helping us to feel what we know is true about us.

When we are functioning from our core value, we feel…

> Regarded *(Romans 8:31-38; Ephesians 1)*
>
> Important *(Psalm 139; Ephesians 1)*
>
> Forgiven *(Ephesians 1:7; Isaiah 43:25; Romans 5:9-11)*
>
> Valued *(Luke 15; 1 Corinthians 7:23)*
>
> Accepted *(Romans 15:7; Romans 5:1-2)*
>
> Powerful *(Ephesians 3:20; Philippians 4:13; 2 Corinthians 12:9; John 16)*
>
> Lovable *(Isaiah 54:10; John 3:16)*
>
> Connected *(John 14:18; Romans 8:38-39)*

Principle 2: Because we live in a broken, fallen world, every person has core hurt.

Because of the presence of sin in the world (Genesis 3; Romans 6–7),

---

* Adapted and reprinted with the permission of The Free Press, a division of Simon & Schuster, Inc., from *You Don't Have to Take It Anymore* by Steven Stosny, PhD. Copyright © 2006 by Steven Stosny. All rights reserved.

we are all fractured at the very core of our person. There is a deep sense of isolation and brokenness in us. Furthermore, because of how others treat us in life (1 John; James) or because of life experiences that are outside of our control (such as deaths or natural disasters), we develop core hurts. Finally, if we have been hurt enough in life, we may develop perceptions about life ("no one cares anyway") that can lead to further core hurt.

When functioning from our core hurt, we feel...

> Disregarded
>
> Unimportant
>
> Accused/Guilty
>
> Devalued
>
> Rejected
>
> Powerless
>
> Unlovable
>
> Separated

When we let ourselves feel our core hurts, they can at times overwhelm us. Core hurts are primary feelings, but when we feel them unexpectedly, they can trigger secondary feelings such as anger or fear that cover the core hurts. Anger or fear feels like the problem, but it is actually a red flag to warn us that we are in our core hurt. The following two graphs show the relationship between anger and core hurts and fear and core hurts.

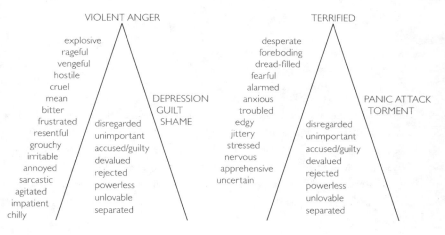

Beginning at the lower left of each triangle, you can see that anger and fear are on a continuum starting with their lesser forms and progressing upward to their more extreme forms. When people explode (violent anger) or are terrified (fear), they eventually come down the righthand side of the pyramids, resulting in other debilitating feelings (depression, guilt, or shame; or panic and torment). They have not really dealt with the deeper problem—their core hurts. The PRAY Process helps people recognize when they are escalating on the pyramid, gives them a tool to interrupt the escalation, shows them what core hurt(s) they have tapped into, and helps them ultimately heal their core hurts through compassion.

Principle 3: As we grow and heal, we can more freely choose to live out of our core value and not out of our core hurt.

The part of the brain I've referred to as the "feeling brain" houses our core values and our core hurts (see chapter 2). Our core values and core hurts are like computer files, side by side, inside that part of our brain.

Core Value	Core Hurt
Regarded	Disregarded
Important	Unimportant
Forgiven	Accused/Guilty
Valued	Devalued
Accepted	Rejected
Powerful	Powerless
Lovable	Unlovable
Connected	Separated

How big each file is (they can be disproportionate) depends on how deeply we know we are valued or how much we've been wounded (Principle 1 and Principle 2 of the PRAY Process). As we grow in life and become more aware of our core value and core hurt, we are better able to make choices about whether to react from our core hurt or live from our core value. While we can't always help what we feel, we can make choices about what to do with our feelings.

Principle 4: As believers, we have the indwelling presence of the Holy Spirit to partner with us in choosing to live out of our core value.

God has not left us alone in this process. As Christians we have the Holy Spirit dwelling in us (Romans 8). The Holy Spirit is described by many words in Scripture, but none so comforting as "helper" (John 16:17). We are encouraged to be filled with the Holy Spirit (Ephesians 5:18). As we partner with the Holy Spirit for character change on the inside, the fruit of the spirit—love, joy, peace, patience, kindness, goodness, faithfulness, gentleness, and self-control—(Galatians 5:23) grows within us. The Holy Spirit is a real presence in us—guiding, strengthening, speaking truth, comforting. As we work through the PRAY Process in the next chapter, it is the Holy Spirit who walks with us, giving us strength and wisdom.

Learning to regulate your feelings from the inside out is like setting the thermostat in your home. Instead of the weather outside dictating how hot or cold it is in your home, the thermostat regulates the temperature so it is comfortable. You are not at the mercy of the weather. In the same way, when you learn to regulate your feelings from the inside through compassion, you are not at the mercy of what happens to you from the outside. You may have difficult people or circumstances in your life, or you may encounter painful life experiences, but you can handle these on the inside in a way that makes all the difference. The steps of the PRAY Process in chapter 4 will guide you as you learn to regulate and manage your feelings from the inside out.

GOING DEEPER:
Understanding Core Value and Core Hurt

1. Which core values and core hurts do you identify with most? Explain.

2. Which "file" in your brain is bigger—your core hurt file or your core value file? Explain.

3. Looking at the anger and core hurts chart and the fear and core hurts chart, which feelings do you identify with most and why?

4. Look up the verses on the "core value" list. What do you feel and think as you read these verses?

5. Write out a few lines acknowledging that your core value is true whether you feel it to be true or not. Read what you wrote to someone you trust, or if you are doing this in a small group, read it to each other. (An example might be, "I don't feel very loveable, but God's Word says I am loved. I am praying that someday I will feel what I know is true about me.")

4

The Steps of
the PRAY Process

The steps of the PRAY Process give you a way to allow God, through the Holy Spirit, into the wounded, hurting places of your heart. It is not a quick fix or a pat formula. To use it that way would be to miss the heart of this whole process, which is the healing of our core hurts through compassion while in the presence of the One who knows us deeply, loves us passionately, and desires our healing and growth more than we do.

Spend a few minutes looking over the chart on page 51. Notice the two square boxes on the left upper half of the chart. You will recognize those as your core hurts and core values. In the middle you see a circle that represents a current problem or event that is touching your life. Sometimes a problem or event happens, but because you are living more from your core value than your core hurt, it doesn't bother you. However, at times your feelings may be triggered by a problem or event and, before you know it, you are angry or afraid and aren't even sure how you got there. The problem triggered your core hurt (which can make you feel shame). You immediately, usually subconsciously, reacted from your core hurt and looked for someone or something outside of yourself to blame. An automatic response to that is trying to protect yourself with anger or with fear, which gives you permission to avoid the problem. Because most people don't know what to do with their anger or fear, they often make poor choices that result in damaging behavior. If that cycle continues, they can end up living a lifestyle of hurt and resentment. This is where the actual steps of the PRAY Process start. If you find yourself in this cycle, you can interrupt it by beginning to recognize when you are angry or afraid and then working through the steps of the PRAY Process.

Once you feel familiar with the PRAY Process chart, you can start walking through each of the steps. You will want to glance back at the chart as you go. Philippians 4:6-7 tells us to "be anxious for nothing, but in everything by prayer and supplication with thanksgiving let your requests be made known to God. And the peace of God, which surpasses all comprehension, shall guard your hearts and your minds in Christ Jesus." This is in no way saying that our worry or anxiety is sin. It is instead a wonderful invitation to us to let our anxiety and worry signal us to pray.

Grounding Event

When some event inside or outside of the self triggers big feelings, usually anger or fear (fight or flight), the brain tends to lock onto these feelings. These feelings can fill all the space inside us in that moment. If we don't *contain* these feelings, they spill over onto others and may cause damage to relationships.

To short-circuit this, we need to refocus the brain by using a form of thought-stopping. When we realize we have a big feeling inside us that is about to spill over onto someone else, we need to **STOP** by doing or thinking something different. This is called a grounding event. It takes the focus off the big feeling and opens the brain for new input. Here are some examples of grounding events:

- See a **STOP** sign flashing in your mind
- Say out loud, "Lord Jesus, have mercy on me" several times
- Describe an object near you out loud
- Leave the room
- Take a walk

Once you have gotten some distance from the "big" emotion, you are ready to proceed with the PRAY Process, where you will learn to partner with God on the inside.

PRAY is an acronym for four steps designed to transform the debilitating feelings that upset your sense of well-being into feelings that bring

The PRAY Process
Philippians 4:6-7

Core Value

regarded	accepted
important	powerful
forgiven	lovable
valued	connected

Problem or Event

Core Hurt

disregarded	rejected
unimportant	powerless
accused/guilty	unlovable
devalued	separated

+ Blame = Protection through anger or fear ➔ Poor choices, damaging behavior ➔ Lifestyle of hurt and resentment

Be angry and sin not (Ephesians 4:26).

or

Perfect love drives out fear (1 John 4:18).

STOP Grounding event to contain and settle the "big" emotions

Process the event through prayer

Reexperience the deepest core hurt

Apply compassion for self and others

You give your attention to the problem

HUDSON/REXIUS © 2006   Adapted from the concepts of Dr. Steven Stosney life—love, peace, joy—by bringing God into the center of your feelings. The steps of PRAY are:

Process the event through prayer

Reexperience the deepest core hurt

Apply compassion

You give your attention to the problem

Step 1: Process the Event Through Prayer

This is where you *observe* and *describe* what just happened. Many people move so quickly in life that to slow down and observe themselves or what is going on around them seems impossible or a waste of time. However, this skill can change the way you live and relate to those you love by causing you to be more thoughtful and less reactive.

To develop this skill, start by asking, "Lord, what just happened?" Think back and observe the internal or external event that occurred and begin to describe it. This is a part of developing the emotional life skill of *self-awareness*. A key element of this step is to do it without judgment. Some people like to describe the event in their head as they pray. Other people like to write their observations down to help them focus.

Describing an event *without* judgment looks like this:

"I was in a hurry, pushing my cart down the aisle of the store. Another person rounded the corner, and our carts collided."

Describing an event *with* judgment looks like this:

"As usual, I was in a hurry, pushing my stupid cart down the aisle of the store when a rather rude person (who wasn't paying attention) ran into my cart."

Judgment distorts and leads to self-criticism or blame of others, which complicates the situation.

Step 2: Reexperience the Deepest Core Hurt

In this step and the next, you develop the emotional skills of *containment of feelings, self-comfort,* and *empathy*.

Ask yourself, "What did I feel?" *Identify* and *feel* your core hurt. This may be difficult because we don't naturally enjoy feeling pain. Look at the "core hurt" list and decide which one or more of the core hurts this event triggered. Then let yourself *feel* the core hurt for 15 to 20 seconds. If you can't feel your core hurts, you will not be able to heal them. In other words, they are not present in order to be healed by compassion. It is important at this point to remind yourself that this is what you *feel*, but it is not *who you are*. For example, you may feel unimportant, but you are not unimportant. Try to avoid self-blame or self-pity.

Step 3: Apply Compassion

This is the most important step in this process. Be kind, nurturing, empathetic, and compassionate with yourself concerning the event. It is important to not judge yourself. Most of us have a "critical voice" inside that is ready to pounce the moment we or someone else "does something wrong." I call this the Pharisee within. We need to replace that voice with a compassionate voice. We need to replace the "Pharisee within" with the "Good Shepherd within." The Pharisee says, "Ha, look what you did. Look at what you feel. Surely you are unlovable." The Good Shepherd says, "Come to me all who are weary and heavy laden and I will give you rest" (Matthew 11:28-30). The Good Shepherd says, "There is no condemnation for you, because you are in Me" (see Romans 8:1).

As you talk to God about the way you were impacted by the event, you can partner with Him to change the negative *meaning* the feeling or feelings give you about yourself. "If I *feel* unlovable that means I *am* unlovable." No! Feelings may be painful, but they do not define you. Only God defines you. You may have a difficult time changing the negative meaning the feeling or feelings give you about yourself at first. Sometimes it helps to talk it through with a friend.

People struggle in this step if what triggered the core hurt was something *they* did rather than something that was done to them that was unkind, insensitive, mean, or wrong. "I don't deserve compassion," they feel. However, the principle remains: What a person does, does not define who they are. You need to confess what you did (1 John 1:9), recognize you made a mistake or a series of mistakes, or actually have a patterned behavior of mistakes, and choose to partner with God to correct this behavior. But this behavior does not mean something *bad* about the self.

As you take time to be compassionate with yourself about how painful your experience has been, you give value to yourself and your experience. This can begin to reconnect you to *feeling* your core value.

Once you are out of the "big" emotions and reconnected to your core value, you are ready to begin solving the problem.

Step 4: You Give Your Attention to the Problem

Relying on God's compassion and using self-compassion to help regulate your emotions does not automatically solve the problem. But having allowed God into the deepest part of your struggle and working with Him to regulate your feelings, you may find yourself feeling more compassionate toward the other person and perhaps better able to see his or her point of view. Often, whatever core hurt you were experiencing is the same core hurt the person with whom you are in disagreement is experiencing. Understanding this can often be very helpful.

From this place of compassion and knowing your core value, you begin to solve the problem. Trying to solve the problem while you are still in your core hurt usually doesn't work. It doesn't work because while you are saying that you want to solve the problem, what you really want is for the other person to make you feel better.

Example 1 of the Steps of the PRAY Process

Grounding event

You have been waiting patiently for a parking space with your turn signal blinking. As the car pulls out of the space you are waiting for, you slowly begin to turn into the space. Suddenly a car comes from nowhere and pulls into "your" space. You go from calm to extreme anger in a moment. You lie on your horn and screech away, yelling, "You idiot!" Finally, you pull into another parking space but are still very angry. You **STOP** and say, "Lord Jesus, have mercy on me!" If you need to, say it several times (a grounding event).

Process the event through prayer

Then ask, "Lord, what just happened?"

You describe what happened without judgment. "I was feeling a little tense because I had been driving all through the parking lot looking for a place to park. I was excited that I finally found a place. I put on my blinker and waited. When the car pulled out of the spot, I started to turn into the empty space. Then out of nowhere, Lord, a car pulled into the space I was waiting for! I got angry, honked my horn, called the guy an idiot, and sped away."

Reexperience the deepest core hurt

"Lord, what is the core hurt under my anger? Am I feeling disregarded, devalued, unimportant, powerless…? Lord, I think I'm feeling disregarded and unimportant."

Let yourself *feel* disregarded and unimportant for 15 to 20 seconds.

"It hurts to feel this, Lord. But I know that even though I'm *feeling* disregarded and unimportant, that is not who I *am*."

Apply compassion

"I don't like it, Lord, when I get so angry at something so relatively small. I'm used to beating myself up for this kind of anger. But I know it's coming from my core hurt—my vulnerability to feeling disregarded and unimportant. Holy Spirit, help me to *feel* what I *know* is true about me—that I am regarded and I am important—to You and to my family and friends. This event, which happened outside of myself with someone I don't even know, can have no meaning regarding my core self. That is safe with You."

You give your attention to the problem

Realizing that you had at first wanted to track the person down in the department store and give him a piece of your mind, you realize that you no longer feel that way and are content to let the incident pass.

Example 2 of the Steps of the PRAY Process

Grounding event

You and your spouse are in a heated conversation about money. You harshly lash out, "I work hard making money, and all you do is spend it! You don't appreciate me at all. Spend! Spend! Spend! You're going to bankrupt us!"

"What do you mean *you* work hard? I work too! Just because I don't make as much as you doesn't make you the boss and judge of how we spend money," your wife yells. "And besides, most of my spending is for the household and the kids, and most of your spending is for your toys! Talk about *me*!"

You yell over her, "Don't you accuse me of being selfish, you stupid…" Fortunately, you catch yourself before you say the last word. "I'm angry. I'm so angry. I need to take a walk." You slam out the front door.

Process the event through prayer

Then ask, "Lord, what just happened?"

You describe what happened without judgment. "My wife and I were arguing about money. That's a common argument. I got angry and accused her of being the problem. She got angry in return and accused me of being the problem. Then I started to call her a name before I caught myself and left the house."

Reexperience the deepest core hurt

"Lord, what is the core hurt under my anger?" You look at the core hurt list. "I think I'm feeling disregarded and accused by my wife. I'm also feeling devalued because of my own behavior. I treated my wife with anger and disrespect."

Let yourself *feel* disregarded, accused, and devalued for 15 to 20 seconds.

"I don't like these feelings, Lord. And I'd rather not feel them. I want to heal. These feelings are real, but they don't define me at my very core. I feel disregarded, accused and devalued, but these feelings are not who I *am*. Help me to not feel sorry for myself or to harshly blame myself."

Apply compassion

"I don't like it, Jesus, when I get so angry at my wife and lash out. I felt my own hurt when she reacted to me out of her hurt. I felt accused and disregarded and covered it with anger. Then I felt devalued when I saw how my behavior and words hurt her. Holy Spirit, help me to not interpret my worth and core value based on my painful feelings. I felt disregarded and accused, but that does not have to define me. Lord, You regard me. You died for me. You love me. I am not accused before You, but forgiven. Even though I made a mistake and lashed out at my wife, that mistake does not take away my value. That is secure with You. Forgive me for letting my anger spill out on my wife. Forgive me for my harsh words that hurt my wife and me. I just want to sit quietly with You for a moment and let Your compassion heal me. It's strange. When I feel Your compassion, I start to feel compassion for myself. Then I find myself feeling compassion for my wife. Thank You."

You give your attention to the problem

Feeling compassion for yourself begins to connect you again to your core value. Not needing your wife to make you feel better, you can now approach her to address the problem. Your wife may or may not have just gone through the same process you did, so you are doing this not for her response but because you want to make things right on your part. There are now two problems—the money discussion and the argument. You discuss the argument first.

"Honey, can I talk to you? When we started talking about money, I lashed out and accused you. Your response resulted in my feeling my core hurts. I felt disregarded and accused. Then I got even angrier and got mean. My own behavior resulted in my feeling devalued. I don't like it when I hurt you or when I hurt myself. I imagine you probably felt some of the same things I did. I'm sorry for both of us. Will you forgive me?"

Depending on her response, you may or may not be able to move on to the other problem—talking about money. Give her time. When she is ready to again talk about money, you could say something like, "I think we see spending money a little differently. If it's okay, could we each give our perspectives about the monthly budget, without criticism, and try again to talk? If it gets too heated, I'm open to having a financial adviser work with us."

Over the years I've taught numerous classes and small groups using the PRAY Process. These are some of the comments I've received:

> "I would go from zero to one hundred with my anger. I didn't think I had any core hurts. But when I began to slow myself down and use the PRAY Process, I discovered I did have

hurt inside. Instead of feeling at the mercy of my anger and everything around me, I've learned to manage my feelings with compassion and, with God's help, heal my core hurts. I never thought I could change, but I have."

"At first, using the PRAY Process didn't feel natural. But after using it for a while, it has become a normal part of my day. I may not use it exactly like the chart shows, but the concept of a grounding event and applying compassion to myself and others has changed the way I relate to my family and friends."

"I've become so much more self-aware. I didn't even know the feelings that were driving me. Now I can identify my feelings and I have a way to heal them."

"I always thought other people caused my feelings. I thought if they would stop doing what they were doing, I wouldn't have to get angry. I sure had that backward. Now I can stop and figure out what's going on inside of me and outside of me and make choices about how I'm going to react."

"Fear used to run my life. As I've begun to focus on healing my core hurts instead of on my fear, my fears have started to lessen. I have a ways to go, but I have a tool to help me when I'm afraid."

Be patient with yourself as you learn to bring the Lord into the wounded places of your heart. His compassion, joined with your "muster seed" of compassion, can heal the painful places inside.

GOING DEEPER:
Understanding the PRAY Process

1. Make a list of possible "grounding events" you could use when your feelings of anger or fear are overwhelming. Share these with someone you trust or with other group members.

2. Reread the **P** of the PRAY Process *(process the event through prayer)*. Try to remember an event from the last week that troubled you. Ask, "What happened?" Try to describe what happened without judgment. Ask others to reflect back to you whether or not your response is judgment free.

3. Reread the **R** of the PRAY Process—*(reexperience the deepest core hurt)*. What core hurt(s) did the above event tap into? Do you know of any reason why?

4. If you can, try to sit quietly with the core hurts you felt for about 20 seconds. What was this experience like? Could you feel them at all? Did they overwhelm you?

5. Reread the **A** of the PRAY Process *(apply compassion)*. How would you apply compassion to the core hurts you just felt? What does it feel like to apply compassion to the core hurts you just felt? Discuss.

6. Reread the **Y** of the PRAY Process (You give your attention to the problem from your core value). How would the above situation look if you tried to resolve it while still in your core hurt? How would it look if you tried to solve it after you've reconnected to your core value?

7. Make several copies of the "PRAY Process Worksheet" (Appendix D) and use it often for the next six weeks. Research indicates it takes up to six weeks to build a new habit.

5

COMPASSION

As I comb through the New Testament, searching for what the heart of the gospel is, I have to conclude that it is the way of compassion. Jesus lived compassion. He touched the untouchable—loved the unlovable. He walked and ate with sinners. He wept over His friend's death. He wept over the condition of people. Over and over again we see Him "moved with compassion." By His life and words He taught that compassion trumps judgment at every turn. Jesus was the embodiment of compassion.

Compassion is what this workbook is about. In the earlier chapters we saw that compassion is integral to growth and healing. Step 3 of the PRAY Process—"apply compassion"—really is at the heart of any genuine healing of our emotions. Yet as I work with clients and teach workshops, I find that this step is the most difficult for people because it involves *feeling*. "Tell me what to do. Tell me how to think. Tell me how to fix it, but don't tell me to *feel* something—that's too vulnerable," they say. Therefore, in this chapter, I would like to explore compassion a little more deeply. For without compassion, we cannot heal and we lose our passion. The way to heal and to rekindle our passion is through finding our heart of compassion. The two are inseparable.

I write about compassion with some trepidation because I so often have failures of compassion in how I relate to myself and to others. My journey with the Lord has been a journey of moving from a more critical, judgmental way of life to a life built more on love and compassion. It is a journey I value deeply.

What Is Compassion?

Compassion is a feeling—a state of being—that allows us to feel empathy for ourselves and for others. It moves us to action on behalf of our own suffering and pain in this world, and it moves us to action on behalf of others' suffering and pain. In conveying the idea of the compassion of Jesus in the New Testament, the writers used phrases such as, "He felt sorry for them," "He was moved with compassion [or pity]," and "His heart went out to them." The Greek word for compassion used in most of these passages conveys a deep emotional reality as well as a physical reaction.

The ability to feel compassion begins early in life. If as children we are treated respectfully, lovingly, and compassionately, compassion begins to grow within us and becomes a part of our character. As we are loved, we learn to love. We learn to feel empathy for ourselves and for others. Throughout life, as we remain open to receiving the love of God and the love of others, compassion stays alive.

Yet compassion is hard. A natural tendency is to become defensive or close our hearts to love and compassion when we have been hurt. And we have all been hurt in life. Compassion is hard because it requires the strength inside to go to the place where we are broken, weak, and lonely and let the love and compassion of God, other people who are safe, and our growing ability to have empathy for ourselves heal us. Compassion is hard because it then requires us to go with others to the place where they are broken, weak, and lonely. Truly we relive the passion of Christ through compassion.

Hindrances to Compassion

Many obstacles hinder compassion in our lives. Following are the two hindrances I hear most often in my office.

Our Wounded Past

When we are hurt in life and don't have a chance to resolve that hurt, our painful feelings have nowhere to go. They get buried inside of us, out of our conscious awareness. The tragedy of this is that over time, if we suppress painful feelings, we also lose touch with feelings that bring life—compassion, love, joy. The first four chapters of this workbook talk about this and give ways to heal from the wounds we experience in life.

An Attitude of Judgment

Probably the deadliest hindrance to compassion is an attitude of judgment toward ourselves and toward others. In our broken, fallen world, we learn at a young age to condemn ourselves when we fail and to condemn others when they fail or act in a "less than perfect" way. Instead of guidance and loving correction, many children are subjected to guilt, shame, or fear as a way of managing their behavior. They have no choice but to learn a self-destructive form of judgment toward themselves and others. "If I fail or make a mistake, I'm all bad and deserve punishment." They beat themselves up emotionally. "If others fail or make a mistake or a series of bad choices, they are all bad and deserve punishment—perhaps banishment." They cut themselves off from whole groups of people they deem "bad." (Do you know that Jesus never squared off with sinners in the New Testament? He sought them out. But He did square off with the religious leaders of His day. They were proud of their own virtues. In fact, they paraded them around for all to see. They were rigid, dogmatic, and judgmental. Jesus confronted their hypocrisy at every turn.) But the above kind of judgment kills the soul! When we judge ourselves with a lack of compassion and understanding, we can't help but judge other people in the same way. When we judge others, it leads right back to judging ourselves. It's a vicious cycle. It deadens our feelings of compassion, and it turns us into what Dallas Willard calls "sin managers." The gospel isn't about sin management—it's about forgiveness, love, transformation, and new life.

Cultivating Compassion

Compassion is an emotional skill that can be developed even if we have wounds from the past or find ourselves judging ourselves or others. Following are ways we can learn to cultivate compassion.

Become Curious

A way out of negative criticism of ourselves and toward others is to cultivate curiosity. Curiosity is a lost art in today's culture. Try asking yourself questions. "I wonder why I needed to lash out in anger just then?" "Why am I so hard on myself at times and then feel sorry for myself at other times?" "I wonder why they think the way they do?" "I wonder what hurt them in the past to make them such a bitter person today?"

Questions such as these can lead us to find out where we hurt—and where others hurt—turning our judgment into compassion over time. Developing curiosity requires slowing down and reflecting. It requires self-awareness.

Risk Becoming Vulnerable

To cultivate compassion we need to become vulnerable. That's hard these days. Being strong, successful, competitive, relevant, powerful—these are the things our culture programs us to seek. We can't get away from that influence. I sometimes deny my vulnerability to that kind of influence. But when I do that, I run the risk of cloaking my desire for these things with a mask of humility. My mask might have the appearance of humility, but in reality I am hiding (even to myself) the drive to be important by the world's standards.

So to risk becoming vulnerable, we look to Jesus...who came in weakness...who came to die...who was gentle and humble...who was led as a sheep to be slaughtered...who hung naked and suffering on a Roman cross. We look to the vulnerable One. When we see Him, we can dare to take off our masks and let Him into the wounded places of our hearts. We can learn to discern safe people and share a bit of our struggle with them. We can quit pretending to be something we're not and just be ourselves. That's freedom. That's when we begin to feel compassion. First we begin to feel compassion for ourselves. Then we begin to feel compassion for others. That's when we find ourselves reaching out to other wounded travelers on this arduous journey of life and together discover that love and mercy and compassion are the strongest forces on earth.

Develop Empathy for Yourself

Another way for us to cultivate compassion is to learn to have empathy for ourselves. For example, whenever I am tempted to criticize myself using negative voices from my past or the negative voices I've created inside my head over the years, I try to stop, sometimes using a "grounding event" such as the ones mentioned in chapter 4. I listen to what that voice is saying and compare it to the voice of Jesus—the Good Shepherd—found in the pages of the Gospels. His voice is gentle. My voice is usually harsh. His voice is comforting. My voice can be condemning. His voice is full of love and compassion. My voice can be judgmental. I recognize that often it is a younger, wounded part of myself that is hurting and lashing out. I attempt to picture myself sitting with Jesus in my favorite place telling Him all that concerns me. As I embrace His voice, I find I begin to have compassion for the person I was who learned to be mean to herself. I see the voices in my head for what they are—attempts to quiet my pain. Sometimes I cry. Sometimes I'm overwhelmed with gratitude for the growth inside over the years. Sometimes I feel Him there. Sometimes I can't feel Him there. If I have a difficult time feeling His presence, sometimes it helps me to quietly play my favorite worship music. If the negative place I'm in gets too overwhelming, I will go talk to a friend who understands this process or to a counselor who can walk me through the painful feelings. But always, He is with me.

Develop Empathy for Others

When we have found a place of compassion in our hearts for ourselves, we can begin to have compassion for others. Actually, these two actions—compassion for self and for others—go hand in hand. If I feel compassion for myself, it opens me up to feel compassion for others. If I feel compassion for others, it circles back and helps me feel compassion for myself. Compassion grows compassion. To feel compassion for others, deep in my heart, I find that I have to "walk a mile" in their shoes. I put myself in their place. I try to think how they think; feel how they feel. I listen. I open my heart to their story. This isn't always easy, and it requires me to "get out of myself" for a bit. But when I do, I usually find a sense of compassion welling up inside. I feel connected to those people in a way that brings meaning to and solidarity with their suffering. Often they say that they don't feel so alone.

I love the story found in the Gospel of John, chapter 8. Jesus was in the temple one day when a group of religious leaders brought a woman caught in the act of adultery to Him. They really weren't interested in this woman—she was simply an object for them to use to trick Jesus. They said that the law of Moses required them to stone her. There she stood, a lone woman in the midst of a group of religious men. How terrifying and humiliating. I've always wondered where the man who was her partner in adultery was. "What do you think, Jesus? Should we stone her?" they asked. Jesus knelt down and began to draw in the sand with His finger. They continued to badger Him. Finally He stood up and said, "He who is without sin among you, let him be the first to throw a stone at her." He knelt back down. Silence. Tension. There she stood. There He was, bent down on His knees. There stood a group of angry men. One by one, from the oldest man to the youngest, they dropped their stones and walked away. Then came the encounter. Jesus stood up and spoke to the woman. She was no longer an object. She was a person.

"Is there anyone left to condemn you?" He said.

"No, Lord, no one," she replied.

"Then neither do I condemn you. Go your way and sin no more."

For many years in my practice as a therapist, part of my work included working with men who battered and with sex offenders. It was difficult not to judge them at first—especially since I came from a sexually abusive background. One evening, while facilitating an advanced group of combined sex offenders and non-protective mothers who were working on their family-of-origin issues, a particular sex offender was recounting the horrible abuse perpetrated on him by his mother. At one point, gripped with agony and unable to talk, he buried his face in his hands. I asked him if I could move closer and put my hand on his shoulder. He nodded yes. When I placed my hand on his shoulder, he surprised me by falling into my arms. I held him as gut-wrenching sobs racked his body. Tears flowed freely in the group that night. The man had been a boy, brutalized by an adult. I had come full circle—the abused comforting the abuser—a gift I will forever cherish. We didn't just learn about compassion that night. We *felt* compassion that night. We were transformed by compassion that night.

No one threw any stones.

GOING DEEPER:
Becoming Compassionate

1. Would you say you are a compassionate person? Why or why not?

2. Do you tend to judge yourself more or others more? Explain.

3. What people bring out the "judgment" part of you?

4. Take a few minutes to "be curious" about why those people think, feel, or act the way they do. If you can, discuss this with others in your group or with a trusted friend.

5. What areas of your life need compassion instead of judgment? What would that look like?

6. Four points on how to cultivate compassion were mentioned: become curious, risk becoming vulnerable, develop empathy for yourself, and develop empathy for others. Which of these areas would you like to grow in? Why?

Afterword

A client sat in my office with tears brimming in her eyes. "I never would have believed that one day I would feel this way," she said. "I used to ask you—demand from you— 'What do I do? How do I fix my feelings?' I was desperate to find something outside of myself to fix me. But instead I've learned to accept myself, in all my good and bad. I've learned that, with God's help on the inside, I can manage my feelings and grow. I've begun to trust the Lord more and actually trust myself. Those two things aren't incompatible. I feel for the first time that I'm living from the inside out and not the outside in. I'm more confident of God's love for me, and I find myself actually experiencing it more often than not. For that I am eternally grateful!"

I believe with all my heart that God wants us to experience His love and compassion in the deepest part of our being. When we do, we begin to walk in this world free. Free from guilt and shame. Free from condemnation and judgment. Free to love ourselves. Free to love others. That's what this workbook is all about—knowing and experiencing God's love. By using the PRAY Process thoughtfully and prayerfully, you can bring God into the painful places of your heart and find His presence there deeply comforting and healing. My prayer is that you would not merely *know* that God is compassionate but that you would *feel* His compassion deep in your heart, and that your compassion for others would grow as a result. When you are able to walk in this way, you will have discovered *compassionate living.*

My hope as you finish this workbook is that these experiences are yours:

- You have a greater understanding of your feelings.

- You understand how you have come to be who you are today.

- You have a tool to process your feelings on a daily basis.

- You have felt compassion.

- You have come to value compassion as the central component of healing.

This journey toward compassionate living is a lifetime process. Be patient with yourself and with others. Take time to cultivate compassion. You will find this investment worth the effort.

This is my prayer for you: "I ask him that with both feet planted firmly on love, you'll be able to take in with all Christians the extravagant dimensions of Christ's love. Reach out and experience the breadth! Test its length! Plumb the depths! Rise to the heights! Live full lives, full in the fullness of God" (Ephesians 3: 17-19 MSG).

May He richly encourage you on your
journey of emotional growth and healing.

Appendix A

Johari Window
Getting to Know Yourself

1. Using the Johari Window, list as many characteristics about yourself as you know and as you know others know about you. This is your "open self" (for example, "I am a friendly person, and others would say that I am friendly").

2. List as many characteristics about yourself as you know but others don't know about you. This is your "hidden self" (for example, "I am uncomfortable meeting new people, but most people don't know that about me because I am friendly").

3. If you feel like taking a little risk, ask people you trust to tell you something about how you come across to them that you might not be aware of. This is your "blind self" (for example, "I see myself as a patient person, but my friends see me as impatient").

4. The "unknown self" is a little more complicated. Discovering the unknown self takes time, so don't expect it to happen overnight (for example, as time goes on you might discover a reservoir of compassion inside of you that you didn't know you had, or you might discover areas of pride of which you were unaware). Ask God to reveal to you deep places of your heart that are unknown to you or to others that might help you to grow. It might be helpful to keep a journal nearby to write down thoughts and feelings that are new to you.

Appendix B

FEELINGS LOG

Take ten minutes at the end of the day to reflect on the feelings you have experienced that day. Check the boxes which indicate the feelings you are aware of having experienced.

Week of _____   **Name** _____

Feelings	Mon.	Tue.	Wed.	Thur.	Fri.	Sat.	Sun.
Adequate							
Angry							
Anxious							
Ashamed							
Bored							
Calm							
Cautious							
Confident							
Confused							
Depressed							
Disgusted							
Ecstatic							
Embarrassed							
Enraged							
Enthusiastic							
Exhausted							
Fearful							
Friendly							
Frightened							
Frustrated							
Furious							
Guilty							

Feelings	Mon.	Tue.	Wed.	Thur.	Fri.	Sat.	Sun.
Happy							
Helpful							
Helpless							
Hopeful							
Hurt							
Hysterical							
Irritated							
Jealous							
Joyful							
Kind							
Lighthearted							
Lonely							
Lovable							
Mischievous							
Numb							
Overwhelmed							
Patient							
Peaceful							
Pleased							
Sad							
Shocked							
Shy							
Surprised							
Suspicious							
Sympathetic							
Trusting							
Other:							
Other:							

Appendix C

Overview of
the Healing Process

The healing process for adults who have experienced some form of trauma as a child is slow. It takes time. Often these people will seem to get worse before they get better. They may even get worse, then better, and then worse again as the process takes its course. The following are stages people *may* go through in the healing process.

Telling the story: This stage involves telling what happened. People need to tell their stories so they do not carry the blame, shame, and guilt.

Owning the truth: This is difficult. No one wants to believe he or she was traumatized or abused as a child, especially if it involved a family member or another significant person. Coming to grips with the truth is necessary before healing can begin.

Validation: In telling their stories, people validate to themselves that the event did happen. It is then important to have "safe" others validate that they believe the event really happened.

Reexperiencing the trauma: As people begin dealing with the trauma, they may experience painful feelings associated with the original trauma. If this does not happen, the feelings stay buried inside and may have an effect on current functioning. Sometimes people repress painful memories. If these memories begin surfacing spontaneously, they may be accompanied by flashbacks, extreme fear, confusion, and other painful feelings. Again, these feelings need to be felt and integrated into the present.

Anger and grief: This is a welcome and normal part of the healing process. It may last for a considerable amount of time.

Confrontation: This may not always be a necessary stage in the healing process, but at the right time and with the right support system, people may need to confront those who harmed them as a means to help empower themselves.

Forgiveness: This is a part of accepting what has happened and eventually letting it go (*not* forgetting it). This seems to be a natural result of having worked through the steps of healing, as well as a conscious choice. To force this too soon shuts down the process. The pain goes into hiding only to surface at a later time.

These stages may not always be present; they may overlap; or the person may go back and forth between stages. The length of time involved depends upon numerous factors, including the severity of the trauma, the age at which it happened, how long it went on, the family environment at the time, the relationship of the offender to the victim, the present psychological maturity of the individual, and his or her present support system. It is not uncommon for the healing process to take a number of years. No two individuals' processes look exactly the same.

Appendix D

STEPS OF THE
PRAY PROCESS WORKSHEET

1. What is my "grounding event"?

2. What are the steps of PRAY?

    P _____

    R _____

    A _____

    Y _____

3. **P**rocess the event. An event has just happened and you are angry or afraid. Describe the event without judgment in the space below or on the back of this page.

4. **R**eexperience the deepest core hurt. What is the core hurt? Identify the core hurt and feel it for 15 to 20 seconds.

5. **A**pply compassion. Write out a prayer on the back of this page that brings the Lord's compassion and your own to bear on the above core hurts (see examples on pages 54-57 for ideas).

6. **Y**ou give your attention to the problem. Is there a problem remaining? What is your part of the problem? What are you going to do about your part of the problem? Write the answer on the back of the page. Pray through the steps above.

ABOUT THE AUTHOR

Jackie Hudson (MS, clinical psychology; MA, biblical studies) is a licensed Marriage and Family Therapist in the state of California and a Licensed Professional Counselor in the state of Oregon. She is currently in private practice in Eugene, Oregon. She also served with Campus Crusade for Christ for 26 years.

ORDER BOOKS

Wipf and Stock Publishers
199 West 8th Avenue, Suite 3
Eugene, OR 97401-2960

Tel: (541) 344-1528
Fax: (541) 344-1506

Website: www.wipfandstock.com

General Inquiries: Info@wipfandstock.com
Ordering Inquiries: Orders@wipfandstock.com